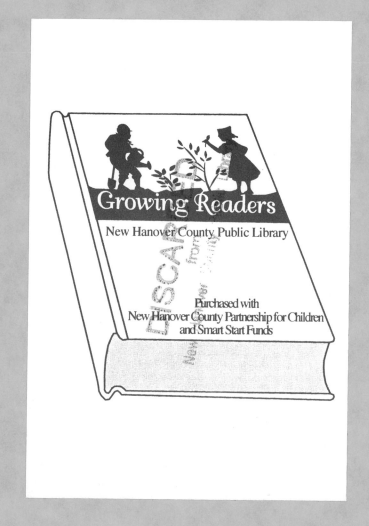

Shapes

Rectangles

by Sarah L. Schuette

Reading Consultant:

Elena Bodrova, Ph.D., Senior Consultant

Mid-continent Research for Education and Learning

A+
Books

A+ Books are published by Capstone Press
P.O. Box 669, 151 Good Counsel Drive, Mankato, Minnesota 56002
http://www.capstone-press.com

1 2 3 4 5 6 07 06 05 04 03 02

Library of Congress Cataloging-in-Publication Data
Schuette, Sarah L., 1976–
    Rectangles / by Sarah L. Schuette.
    p.cm—(Shapes)
    Summary: Simple text, photographs, and illustrations show rectangles in everyday objects.
    Includes bibliographical references and index.
    ISBN 0-7368-1462-0 (hardcover)
    I. Rectangle—Juvenile literature. [1.Rectangle.] I. Title.
QA482 .S38 2003
516'.15—dc21
                                                                    2002000893

Created by the A+ Team

Sarah L. Schuette, editor; Heather Kindseth, art director and designer; Jason Knudson,
    designer and illustrator; Angi Gahler, illustrator; Gary Sundermeyer, photographer;
    Nancy White, photo stylist

Note to Parents, Teachers, and Librarians

The Shapes series uses color photographs and a nonfiction format to introduce children to the shapes around them. It is designed to be read aloud to a pre-reader or to be read independently by an early reader. The images help early readers and listeners understand the text and concepts discussed. The book encourages further the following sections: Table of Contents, Words to Know, Read More, Internet Sites, and Index. Early readers may need assistance using these features.

Table of Contents

4

Rectangles have four sides, two short and two long.

Everyone makes mistakes. Luckily, you can easily fix mistakes on your homework with an eraser.

They rub out the answers you write that are wrong.

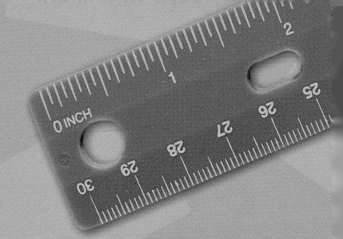

Rectangles can measure
and draw straight lines.

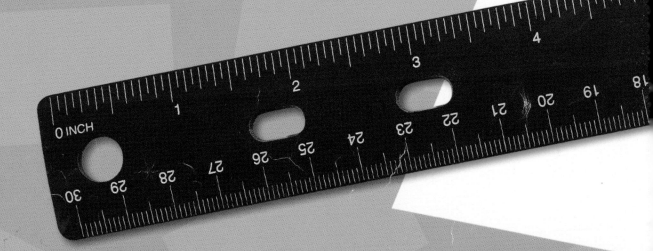

Speed limit signs tell drivers about safe speeds. Traffic signs come in many different shapes and colors.

Rectangles are white speed limit signs.

Fifty-two rectangles
make up a deck.

13

Happy Birthday

On your birthday, you might get a check.

Banks will give you money when you exchange a check for cash. Then you can save your money or buy a fun treat.

You use rectangles
when you pay.

Did you know that most pianos have 88 black and white keys? Musical notes tell players which keys to press on the piano. Some piano players can even play without reading music.

Piano keys are rectangles you play.

19

$$8$$
$$-4$$

$$8 + 4 =$$

$$aA$$

$$+2$$

$$5 + 2 = 7$$

$$bB$$

$$2 \times 3 = 6$$

Use flash rectangles
at your school.

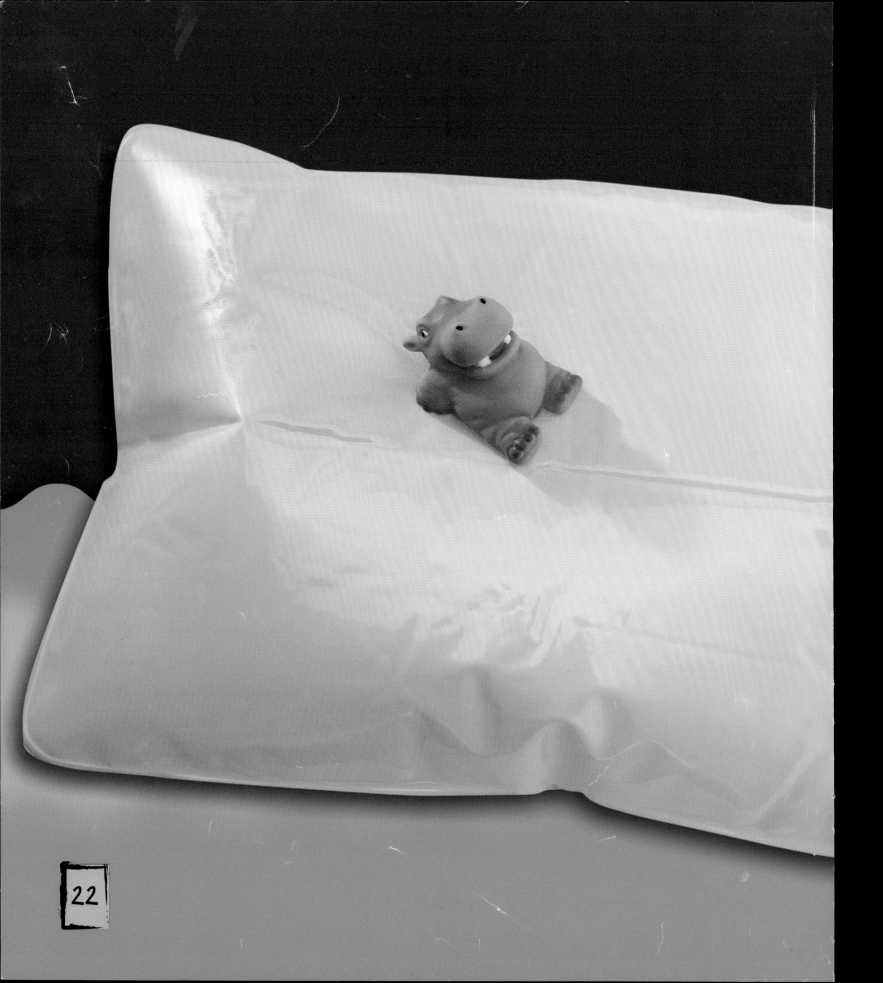

A rectangle can even float in your pool.

It is fun to chew gum and blow bubbles. If you ever get gum stuck in your hair, use peanut butter to get it out.

Sticks of gum are rectangles you chew.

Find the rectangle that sticks on you.

26

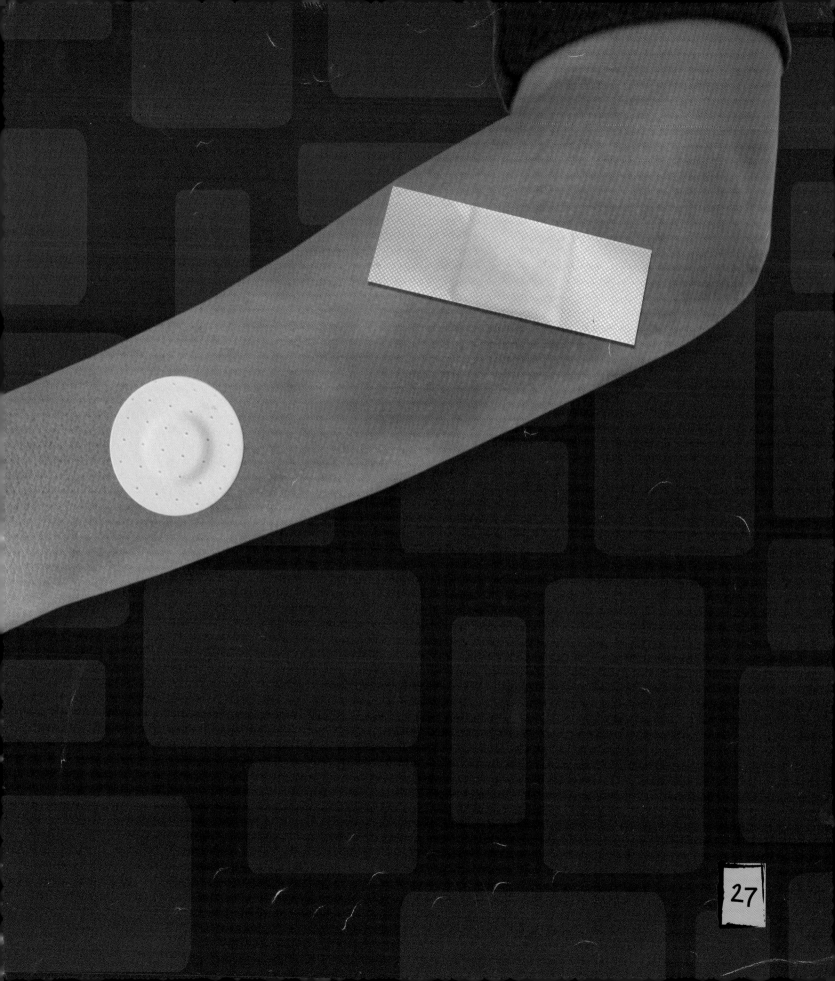

Build a Rectangle Town

You will need

graham crackers

cookie sheet

tubes of frosting

plastic spoon

colored sprinkles

gel icing

SNAP!

1 Break a few of the large crackers into smaller rectangle pieces. Arrange the pieces on the cookie sheet.

2 Spread the frosting on the crackers with the spoon. Add sprinkles.

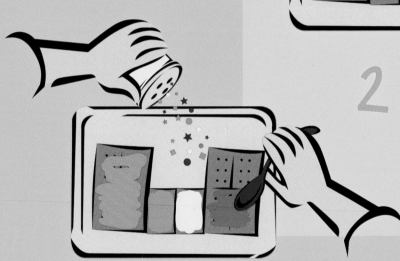

3 Draw windows and doors with the gel icing. Try making other rectangles that you see in your town.

29

Words to Know

deck—a full set of playing cards; there are 52 cards in a deck; each card is a rectangle.

exchange—to give one thing and to get something back in return; people can exchange checks for cash at banks.

measure—to find out the size of something; rulers are rectangles that people use to measure or draw straight lines.

note—a written symbol that stands for a musical sound

piano—a large keyboard instrument; pressing down on the black and white keys on a piano makes different sounds.

speed—the rate that something moves; speeds can be slow or fast; speed limit signs are rectangles.

Read More

Burke, Jennifer S. *Rectangles.* City Shapes. New York: Children's Press, 2000.

Patilla, Peter. *Starting Off with Shapes.* Hauppauge, New York: Barron's, 2001.

Ross, Kathy. *Kathy Ross Crafts Triangles, Rectangles, Circles, and Squares.* Learning Is Fun! Brookfield, Conn.: Millbrook Press, 2002.

Yates, Irene. *All about Shapes.* New York: Benchmark Books, 1998.

Internet Sites

Track down many sites about rectangles.
Visit the FACT HOUND at *http://www.facthound.com*

IT IS EASY! IT IS FUN!

1) Go to *http://www.facthound.com*
2) Type in: 0736814620
3) Click on "FETCH IT" and FACT HOUND will find
   several links hand-picked by our editors.

Relax and let our pal FACT HOUND do the research for you!

Index